BEFORE

YOU

SAY "I DO"

Revised and Expanded

Dare to open the lid and see inside or what you don't see is what you will get.

[Gen. 2:24] Therefore shall a man leave his father and his mother, and shall cleave unto his wife: and they shall be one flesh.

By Gilbert James
Dedicated To My Daughter,
Gilline James

Into Thine Hand
4141 NW 39th Ave
Fort Lauderdale FL 33309
www.intothinehand.com

TABLE OF CONTENTS

The Lovers Calendar

January Is The Beginning Of Each Calendar Year
The Time To Treat Your Love With Tender Loving Care
The Month After January, Love Birds, Is February
Make Sure Your Love Bond Is Strong And Stationary
March Is The Month That Comes In Third
Please Speak Your Love To The One Your Heart's Preferred
April Is The Month To Give Lovers Thrills
Make Sure You Give Them In Diverse Love Bills
No Love Decay, Month May Is Not Here To Stay
Give Love In A Vase And Give Your Heart Away
The Month After May, Vandal, Is June
The Month Your Love Cords Should Be Set In Tune
Take It Or Leave It, We're Now In July
The Month You Should Die To Let Your Love Fly High
Month August Like Dust Has Sneaked Upon Our Bust
Let's Give All That's In Us To Worth Our Partner's Trust
Stick, Stone Or Timber, We Are Now In Month September
Let's All Get Together And Make This A Time To Remember
The Month Of October Has Now Taken Over
Please Be Thou Sober And So Think Things Over
Take Stock You Love Offender, We Are Now In Month
November
Irrespective Of Your Sex Or Gender, Be This Month, A Surprise
Sender
Hi There You Love Pretender, Please Remember, It Is December
Tough You Have Been Your Love Contender, This Month Be
Your Love Defender

Send The Gift Of Love

Gift Sender /Receiver Page

From Your:

❑ Wife ❑ Husband ❑ Prospective Husband ❑ Prospective Wife ❑ Fiance ❑ Fiance to be ❑ New girlfriend ❑ New boyfriend ❑ The one who loves you the most ❑ Other _____

Print Name: _____ Signature: _____

To My:

❑ Wife ❑ Husband ❑ Prospective Husband ❑ Prospective Wife ❑ Fiance ❑ Fiance to be ❑ New girlfriend ❑ New boyfriend ❑ The one who loves you the most ❑ Other _____

Print Name: _____ Signature: _____

Dedicated to:

❑ My love for you ❑ Our *Marriage* ❑ Our Anniversary ❑ Our engagement ❑ Our engagement to be ❑ Our continuing friendship ❑ The continuing unity of our relationship ❑ Other _____

MY PERSONAL LETTER
"My love for you is heated a thousand times the highest number"

The Greatest Love

THE GREATEST LOVE
Greater love hath no man than this, that a man
lay down his life for his friends.
[John 15:13]

CHAPTER 1

Singleness Is a Divine Loan

You can see a loan as a source of reckless spending, secure saving or vested investing.

Getting Really Personal
Honesty Is Reality. How Much Of It Can You Face Head On?

So you are single, meaning that you are not married? If the answer is yes, so what, but on the other hand, why? Who or what is responsible for this heinous crime of you still being a solo team? Is this your choice? Is it because you are not prepared for the change of status? Are you sure that you are going about it the right way? Most importantly, is this what God wants for you?

In the first place, what is wrong with being single, not being married? You may say that even the creator said from the beginning that it is not good for mankind to be alone. But are you really alone? And if so, whose fault is it? With over five billion creatures like yourself on this planet, yea your planet, is something radically wrong if you still find yourself alone? With the perpetual availability of one who is always ready and willing to be your friend, Jesus Christ, can you still blame anyone else, if you find yourself still alone today?

Even society, as it becomes more civilized and developed, tells you that you have to be a little on the insane side if you are of full age and still not married, you respond.

You continue: "Are you fully aware that upon my revelation of my

11

single or not married status, the obvious question is something wrong with me instead of with them?" The natural inclination is that something has to be wrong with me, instead of the masses.

Getting Really Sober

"Take A Stand On The Facts." The Fiction, Yours Or Theirs, Flush!

Does that make it true? What makes you think that the crowd cannot be wrong? In fact, a careful study of the history of mankind reveals that the masses have been wrong most of the times.

They were wrong in the garden of Eden when the entire population of mankind participated in the partaking of the forbidden fruit.

They were wrong in the days of Noah when only eight out of the population of the entire world (God knows how many) were right. As a result, they were the only ones who chose to enter the ark and be saved from the world flood.

They were wrong in the case of Lot when the big cities of Sodom and Gomorrah became the choice of Lot and his family. Abraham and his family, on the other hand, chose the seemingly "actionless" portion with the presence and power of God in their choice. On that occasion, the same Abraham had pleaded for Lot with the angels of God who were about to destroy the apparently well watered cities of Sodom and Gomorrah with Lot and the rest of its occupants. Out of the entire population of the two cities, only three people were saved... Lot and his two daughters.

They were wrong throughout the life of the children of Israel where God had only been able to use a remnant of the entire nation down through her history.

They have proven themselves wrong in choosing the way of destruction over life eternal. *Matthew 7:13 ...broad is the way, that leadeth to destruction, and many there be which go in thereat.*

History shows that they have been wrong in prioritizing, diagnosing and choosing most things that really count. So why should you think that this is the end of the world just because the crowd says that something is wrong with you? Do you realize that the crowd follows the crowd? Are you aware that the crowd cheers with the crowd? Do you know that opportunists can always be bought with a more attractive offer without that offer necessarily being in line with a predetermined mission?

If one chooses to remain single, is that recommended? Can anything possibly be right about being single or becoming of full age and not being married?

Surprisingly, there are many things that are right about being single.

In the first place, 'it is good, or ok' ...*It is good for a man not to touch a woman. 2. Nevertheless, to avoid fornication, let every man have his own wife, and let every woman have her own husband. [1 Corinthians 7:1-2]* The word touch means to fasten one's self to or be joined to. The concept presented here is that of a union, commitment or a binding agreement.

The inclusion of both genders in verse two of first Corinthians seven reveals that both the male and female are being addressed here.

Therefore a proper interpretation of the passage would be that it is good for a person not to touch {joined or fastened to} a mate but to avoid fornication, let every man have his own wife and every woman have her own husband.

Verse eight of first Corinthians seven tells us that *it is good* for the unmarried and widows if they abide as the apostle Paul was (not married). *"I say therefore to the unmarried and widows, It is good for them if they abide even as I."*

Verses twenty-five and six of first Corinthians seven say that it is good for a virgin so to be. *"25. Now concerning virgins I have no commandment of the Lord: yet I give my judgment, as one that hath obtained mercy of the Lord to be faithful. 26. I suppose therefore that this is good for the present distress, I say, that it is good for a man so to be."*

Verse thirty-seven of 1st Corinthians seven tells us that if you so decree that you will keep your virginity, you do well. *"Nevertheless he that standeth stedfast in his heart, having no necessity, but hath power over his own will, and hath so decreed in his heart that he will keep his virgin, doeth well."*

In the second place, a single person cares for the things of the Lord more than if you were married. First Corinthians seven verses thirty two through thirty four tell us that the unmarried cares for the things of the Lord, how he/she might please the Lord. But the married cares for the things of the world, how he/she might please his/her spouse. *"32. But I would have you without carefulness. He that is unmarried careth for the things that belong to the Lord, how he may please the Lord: 33. But he that is married careth for the things that are of the world, how he may please his wife. 34. There is difference also between a wife and a virgin. The unmarried woman careth for the things of the Lord, that she may be holy both in body and in spirit: but she that is married careth for the things of the world, how she may please her husband."*

The "single" [not married] can share a union with God that very rarely is matched again after marriage. I remember a time when I was getting very close to a friend and I got very scared. The reason was that I felt backslidden within my heart just to share the closeness that I had with God with someone else. I felt that I was losing my 'undistracted' union that I had with God by getting close to this friend.

As a single person, you can accomplish your spiritual as well as life's goals without unreasonable distraction. One reason being… you do not have to have second thoughts about a spouse when you are planning to reach your future goals. If you are married, biblically, your spouse comes second to God and first over everything and everyone else. As a married person, you are restricted. You are obligated to your spouse and the goals that you can accomplish as a family.

Do you know how many potential geniuses have eclipsed their

future because of silly anxiety or curiosity to say "I DO?" The list is long, and will continue to expand. But the question now is who will be next on that list? Will it be you?

Remember that it was the same aspiration and anxiety, yea, curiosity without giving consideration to the eminent consequence that got our first mother and father, thus the whole human race into this mess that we are in today.

Is it really worth it to allow anxiety or curiosity, yea, greed to dictate your future? It is not worth it to ruin an entire life's potential in one moment, day, week, month or even year's time.

Getting Really Offensive
"Destroy The Snake Under Your Grass."
You Could Be Protecting The Killer Of Your Fields

So you are still single... and whose fault is it? The world, as well as you, yourself are asking you this question, "why are you still not married?" In short, who or what is responsible for this heinous crime of you still being a solo team? Is it because that's what you want? Or is it not? What you want means that you choose over anything and anyone else to remain the way you are, not married. If you are this way by choice, you are ranked in a category which very few of the people holding a single status have successfully held. You, in contrast to very few others, can shout it from the house top, proudly, (I hope) "I am this way because this is my choice. I am in control of my personal life or destiny." And you should be commended for having been able to exercise, so far, your power of choice.

Thus, you should not only be aware of, but also should be man or woman enough to own up to the fact that you have no one else to blame for your status but you, including the pain and, or gain of such status.

If you are forced to remain this way as a result of rejection, it doesn't roll many points into your corner. It could mean that you have much polishing to do to yourself. Being in this status could mean that you are regulated by the people whom you value as valuable. It is also possible that you allow yourself to be enslaved by them. And believe it or not, it could also mean that your prospects cannot perceive what is true value based on their level of evaluation. If so, this could throw many points in your corner. This would mean that the defect, if not defects, is with them instead of you. This would mean that you should give yourself some credit instead of discredit.

It could also mean that you are a jewel, and probably were not aware of it. This could also mean that you are ranked in a higher bracket than your prospects. Therefore you should feel honored because you might be too good for them, so to speak. God might have someone better for you.

The possibility also exists that you are this way because you need to reconstruct your strategy. In the first place, your method of searching might need to be right side up. The biblical strategy is as follows: *Seek ye first the kingdom of God and His righteousness and all these things shall be added unto you [Matthew 6:33].* This should be understood quite clearly that the kingdom of God is referring to salvation or the new birth. Jesus said that except a man be born again, he cannot even see the kingdom of God.   He also went on to show that being born again is the requirement for entering into the kingdom of God *{John 3:3, 5}.* Therefore, you should first seek to be ready for the kingdom or be born again. Next you must seek the righteousness of God. In short, you must seek after righteous living.

Titus 2:12 says that *"teaching us that denying ungodliness and worldly lust, we should live soberly, righteously and godly in this present world."* To live righteously, we must deny ungodly and worldly lust. And this must come before you search for a mate. Please don't get mad at me, I am not the one who said it, the Bible says it. It is a super great possibility that your answer lies right in this ball park. You should probably play in it some more. You might very well come out scoring greatly.

In the second place, your concept of love might need to be restructured. Jesus   said: *"Here in is the great commandment fulfilled: Love the Lord thy God with all thy heart, with all thy soul, and with all thy mind; and thou shall love thy neighbor as thyself"* *{Matthew 22:37-38}.* According to this passage, your love should be first directed to God, second, yourself, and third, your neighbor.

This passage clearly tells us that we must first fall in love with God. And if you notice further, you will see that we must love our neighbors as ourselves. Love for ourselves must come before our love for our neighbors. We must first set up a pattern of how much we will love our neighbors by how much we are able to love ourselves.

If we cannot truly and effectively love ourselves, we cannot truly and effectively love our neighbors. Therefore it is evident that second to God, we must first seek to truly and effectively love ourselves, respect ourselves, dream of the best for ourselves, have respect to our needs, treat ourselves with the best, especially some TLC [tender loving care], then we will thus be able to share this love with our neighbors in the same manner.

Some people love themselves first, God second and others last. Some love their mates first, themselves second, and God last. I submit to you that both of these structures need to be completely restructured. The right structure is God first, yourself second and your neighbors third. The truth is that you cannot truly love you until you truly are able to love God. And you cannot truly love your mate or your neighbor until you truly are able to love you. With this same token, if you can truly love God, you will truly be able to love yourself. And if you can truly love yourself, you will truly be able to attract and love your present or future mate and your neighbors.

Finally, it is highly possible that, your single status is what God wants for you. In *Matthew 19:12* Jesus said that there are *some eunuchs who were made so from birth.* No man but the master has any control over that. This means that God made some eunuchs from birth. That is by His divine providence, not by choice.

The word eunuch does not only mean being barren, not able to have children. According to the different uses in Scripture, it refers to someone who remains without an intimate relationship with the opposite sex.

17

It also refers to someone who has notable abilities and is totally unattached to anything or anyone who will slow or stop him/her from putting those abilities to full use. Examples of this can be found first, in *2 Kings 20:18 "And of thy sons that shall issue from thee, which thou shalt beget, shall they take away; and they shall be eunuchs in the palace of the king of Babylon."*

Second, God told Jeremiah in *Jeremiah 16:2* that he should not take to himself a wife in that place and at that time. *"Thou shalt not take thee a wife, neither shalt thou have sons or daughters in this place."* Whatever the reason might have been, at least for that time and out of that place he was not to take unto him a mate.

Another example of the use of the word eunuch is found in the book of *Daniel 1:9*, where Daniel, himself was a eunuch *"Now God had brought Daniel into favour and tender love with the prince of the eunuchs."* I have not found any record where Daniel was attached to any wife or had children. It is evident from the scriptures that he was fully freed of any one and anything that would prevent him from fully carrying out his commissioned conviction or course of life.

CHAPTER 2

Biblical Reasons for Getting Married or Remaining Single

It is better to marry than to burn. However, is it always better to marry? Let us see what the Scripture says.

For this chapter, we will primarily examine 1 Corinthians 7. We will explore the following outline found in the chapter:

- The apostle Paul devoted a substantial number of verses from this chapter to the basis for remaining single and also the basis for getting married.
- He also devoted a noticeable portion of this chapter to the behavior on both sides of the chart: singleness vs marriage.
- Finally, he devoted a good portion of the chapter to the benefit and setbacks of both singleness and marriage.

The premise of the chapter is presented to us in the apostle Paul's own words, as he responded to questions that were addressed to him by the church of Corinth: *1 Corinthians 7:1a "Now concerning the things whereof ye wrote unto me."* Notice that the apostle Paul classified the issues that the Corinthian church addressed to him in the plural form *"things"*, which means that he wasn't just referring to the first question that he answered in verse 1-2. It is quite likely that the entire chapter 7 was taken up with the issues that the Corinthian church wrote to the apostle Paul. Notice additionally that he specified clearly that he was addressing the *questions that they wrote* unto him which means that he did not impose these issues upon them and provide

19

answers to them in this instance, though that was not uncommon or unethical. He has done that in all of his epistles. These issues were real questions regarding singleness and marriage that the Corinthian church had. The questions that the Corinthian church had were no different to similar, if not identical questions that our churches have today, if we were to be honest with ourselves. Thirdly, these are questions that we as individual believers have too.

Let us look, first of all, at the bases for remaining single and the bases for getting married. In verses 1-2 he presented the first basis as: To avoid or prevent fornication. 1. *"...It is good for a man not to touch a woman. 2. to avoid fornication, let every man have his own wife, and let every woman have her own husband."* The word used for *"good"* in this passage is the word ἄπιστος apistos which means meet, fit, appropriate or expedient. The word used for *"man"* here, though not explicit, is implicit, that not only the male is addressed but also the female. The context lends itself to the 'implicity' of both genders being addressed here. In other words an insertion of vice versa is justifiably present. The answer to this is found in verse two where both the male and the female are included: *let every man have his own wife, and let every woman have her own husband.*

This is why it would be a misinterpretation of the passage to limit the word touch used here to just a male touching a female. The English word *"touch"* used in this passage comes from the Greek word ἄπτομαι (haptomai) which means *to be joined or fastened.*

What this is actually saying is that it is meet, fit, appropriate or expedient to remain single (not *joined or fastened to the opposite sex.* There is nothing wrong with it. As a matter of fact, later on down in the chapter, he specified that it may even be better spiritually, to remain single. We see this in verses *32-33:* "*32 ...He that is unmarried careth for the things that belong to the Lord, how he may please the Lord: 33 But he that is married careth for the things that are of the world, how he may please his wife.* It is also repeated in verses 37-38: *37 Nevertheless he that* *standeth stedfast in his heart, having no necessity, but hath power over his own will, and hath so decreed in his heart that he will keep his **virgin**, doeth well. 38 So then he that giveth her in marriage doeth well; but he that giveth her not in marriage doeth better.* The word **virgin** in verse 37 refers to ones **virginity**.

However, it is also meet, fit, appropriate or expedient to be married, and from the apostle Paul's own words, it could be even better to be married. We see this in verse 9: *"But if they cannot contain, let them marry: for IT IS BETTER TO MARRY THAN TO BURN.*

The basis that he provided us for getting married in verses 1-2 of 1 Corinthians is *"to avoid or prevent fornication."* By avoiding and preventing here, he speaks to both those of *us who are tempted to begin committing fornication* and those of *us who are already involved in fornication.*

I truly don't believe that the apostle Paul is exhorting us to grab every or any Tom, Dick or Harry that we lay eyes upon and propose or push marriage out of a mission to avoid fornication. However, if you are involved with someone that you love and you are either on the verge of committing fornication or are already involved in fornication, the remedy for avoiding or preventing a life of fornication is to get married.

The next basis that the apostle Paul provided for marriage is to avoid or prevent burning (if you cannot contain) and for remaining single: for the Gospel sake. Here is what verses *7-9 tells us: "7 For I would that all men were even as I myself. But every man hath his proper gift of God, one after this manner, and another after that. 8 I say therefore to the unmarried and widows, It is good for them if they abide even as I. 9 if they cannot contain, let them marry: for it is better to marry than to burn."* It is believed that the apostle Paul led a single life throughout all of his tenure as an apostle for the Lord or at least most of it. Listen to his own words in *1Corinthians 9:3-5 3 Mine answer to them that do examine me is this, 4 Have we not power to eat and to drink? 5 Have we not power to lead about a sister, a wife, as well as other apostles, and as the brethren of the Lord, and Cephas?*

There are scholars who propose that the apostle Paul was married. One of the passages that they use to prove that is verse *8 of 1 Corinthians 7,* where he made reference to the unmarried and widows remaining as he was. From this they surmise that he either was widowed or unmarried, which is to be loose from a wife. The deduction here is that he didn't classify himself as single but rather, widowed or unmarried.

However, let's not be so quick to conclude that he was unmarried or divorced. Let us take note that he used the same term: "unmarried" to refer to all those who are not married in verses *32-34 of 1 Corinthians 7: "32 ...He that is unmarried careth for the things that belong to the Lord, how he may please the Lord: 33 But he that is married careth for the things that are of the world, how he may please his wife. 34 There is difference also between a wife and a virgin. The unmarried woman careth for the things of the Lord, that she may be holy both in body and in spirit: but she that is married careth for the things of the world, how she may please her husband."*

Notice that he made a distinction between the wife and the virgin in verse 34. A wife can never be a virgin again, even when she is loosed from her husband. Notice also in verse 35, that both the virgin and those loosed from a husband are classified under the one "unmarried" umbrella as those women who are not wives. He further went on to classify the wives as "she that is married."

The apostle Paul in 1 Corinthians 9:5 wipes out the claim to mandatory celibacy for the pastorate or the disciples (apostles) including the apostle Paul. *"Have we not power to lead about a sister, a wife, as well as other apostles, and as the brethren of the Lord, and Cephas?"*

The word "we" used by the apostle Paul here is in reference to the apostle Paul speaking for all of the apostles or clergy men.

Having the power means duly, biblically authorized. The term "lead about" is referring to having a married companion. One could also look at this passage and say that he mentioned "a sister" which denotes generalization as if he had the right to have a church sister or sisters on his team. However, the context lends itself to the construct of the discussion of a marriage partner. The term *"wife"* used could also denote him having the right to attach a wife to his ministry or himself.

Another argument used to prove the apostle Paul with a married status (at least at some point) is the fact that he was a member of the Sanhedrin, which requires that their members be married, at least in the early existence of that sect.

Another deduction used to establish that the apostle Paul was married is the fact that he was a Pharisee. We see this confirmed in *Acts 23:6 But when Paul perceived that the one part were Sadducees, and the other Pharisees, he cried out in the council, Men and brethren, **I am a Pharisee, the son of a Pharisee:** of the hope and resurrection of the dead I am called in question. Philippians 3:5 Circumcised the eighth day, of the stock of Israel, of the tribe of Benjamin, an Hebrew of the Hebrews; as touching the law, **a Pharisee;***

It is my position that whether he was married or not, he spent most, if not all of his life as an apostle as a single person. At least, at the time when he was speaking in 1 Corinthians 7, he was single because **He placed himself in the category of those who were not married in that chapter.**

Some even proposed that he forfeited his wife's for the Gospel sake. However, if there is any forsaking, it would be on the wife side due to his total devotion to the work of God. Listen to his own words which reflects his own position regarding spousal abandonment. In 1 Corinthians 7:5 *Defraud ye not one the other, except it be with consent for a time, that ye may give yourselves to fasting and prayer; and come together again, that Satan tempt you not for your incontinency.*

23

He expressed his total disdain for spousal abandonment again in 1 Corinthians 7:12-15 - *12 But to the rest speak I, not the Lord: If any brother hath a wife that believeth not, and she be pleased to dwell with him, let him not put her away. 13 And the woman which hath an husband that believeth not, and if he be pleased to dwell with her, let her not leave him. 14 For the unbelieving husband is sanctified by the wife, and the unbelieving wife is sanctified by the husband: else were your children unclean; but now are they holy. 15 But if the unbelieving depart, let him depart. A brother or a sister is not under bondage in such cases: but God hath called us to peace.*

Getting back to the basis for getting married being to avoid or prevent burning (if you cannot contain), examine the following: Cannot contain means cannot be temperate or maintain self control. To burn literally means to be on fire or to be in fury. Laughter: What this is saying is that if a cold shower or locking yourself into the freezer can't help you, then get married. You are beyond repair... your only biblical solution is to get married.

On the contrary, just like the apostle Paul remained celibate for the Gospel sake, you can choose that route also, which is also meet, fit, appropriate or expedient. Some people are gifted like that, though I don't believe that the desire is taken away. *Matthew 19:12 For there are some eunuchs, which were so born from their mother's womb: and there are some eunuchs, which were made eunuchs of men: and there be eunuchs, which have made themselves eunuchs for the kingdom of heaven's sake. He that is able to receive it, let him receive it.*

From the womb: Such as are naturally incapable of marriage, and consequently should not contract any. —*Adam Clarke's Commentary.*— Persons constitutionally either incapable of or indisposed to marriage. —*JFB Commentary*— It's natural for those born with diminished sexual desire to remain unmarried. —*Tony Evans Bible Commentary*— I, the author believe that this could also include a physical or mental disability like a handicap person with either a physical or mental handicap or both.

Dare to open the lid and see inside

By Men: A position, profession like an eunuch or even castration is being proposed here, like a 'cupbearer' in the Bible. By voluntary choice: They still need the grace of God to maintain their singleness.

Here is the apostle Paul in his own words: *[1 Corinthians 9:27]* I keep under my body, and bring it into subjection: lest that by any means, when I have preached to others, I myself should be a castaway. *[Romans 7:21]* I find then a law, that, when I would do good, evil is present with me. It is not seen in scripture where Nehemiah or Daniel carried about a wife because they held an extremely critical position in their service to the king. This is also seen in Acts 8 where the Ethiopian authority who served directly under Queen Candace was an Eunuch.

The third basis for singleness presented by the apostle Paul is "the present distress" and for marriage is "it is not a sin or sinful" *1 Corinthians 7:25-28* *²⁵concerning virgins I have no commandment of the Lord: yet I give my judgment, as one that hath obtained mercy of the Lord to be faithful. ²⁶I suppose therefore that this is good for the present distress, I say, that it is good for a man so to be. ²⁷Art thou bound unto a wife? seek not to be loosed. Art thou loosed from a wife? seek not a wife. ²⁸and if thou marry, thou hast not sinned; and if a virgin marry, she hath not sinned. Nevertheless such shall have trouble in the flesh: but I spare you.*

Adam Clarke's Commentary: The word αναγκη anankē, used for distress, signifies necessity, distress, tribulation, and calamity; as it does in *Luke 21:23; 2 Corinthians 6:4; 12:10.* In such times, when the people of God had no certain dwelling place, when they were lying at the mercy of their enemies without any protection from the state—the state itself often among the persecutors—he who had a family to care for, would find himself in very embarrassing circumstances, as it would be much easier to provide for his personal safety than to have the care of a wife and children. On this account it was much better for unmarried persons to continue for the present in their celibacy.

25

Carry the least amount of distress into the marriage as you can: The more baggage that you can get rid of before transferring them over into the marriage, the better your married lives will be. In actuality, you would only translate them into the marriage.

Don't get married as a motive to solve your depressing situation. It would likely continue or get worst in the marriage. Try to resolve as much of your distresses prior to the marriage.

Don't get married as an answer to your lack of self control, it would likely continue or get worst in the marriage. For the most part, other than sexual constraints, marriage will not solve your self control issues. That needs to be taken care of prior to the marriage.

Don't get married as a motive to resolve your laziness or lack of ambition to achieve… marriage requires a lot of the opposite qualities: Hard work and highly ambitious achievements for the family are among the fuel that marriage requires to keep the fire burning, so to speak.

The less debt or unsustainable debt that you can carry over into the marriage, the better chance your marriage has for survival. IF YOU ARE IN DISTRESS financially, emotionally, vocationally, personally or otherwise, your best option is to try as much as possible to get as much of those issues resolved before entering into marriage with them. They could be disastrous to the marriage.

Loose from a wife… What does that mean? Is divorce or all divorces a biblical basis for being loosed from a spouse?

Divorce was first introduced or allowed by Moses and based on Jesus' words, Moses inserted it as an improvisational option due to the hardness of man's heart. *Deuteronomy 24:1-2 1. When a man hath taken a wife, and married her, and it come to pass that she find no favour in his eyes, because he hath found some uncleanness in her: then let him write her a bill of divorcement, and give it in her hand, and send her out of his house. 2. when she is departed out of his house, she may go and be another man's wife.*

Jesus classified it as *not so from the beginning* and from my understanding of Jesus's response to this issue, He has never deviated from that position, including the exception clause in *Matthew 19:3-11.* *"The Pharisees also came unto him, tempting him, and saying unto him, Is it lawful for a man to put away his wife for every cause? 4 And he answered and said unto them, Have ye not read, that he which made them at the beginning made them male and female, 5 Amd said, For this cause shall a man leave father and mother, and shall cleave to his wife: and they twain shall be one flesh? 6Wherefore, they are no more twain, but one flesh. What therefore God hath joined together, let not man put asunder. 7 They say unto him, Why did Moses then command to give a writing of divorcement, and to put her away? 8 He saith unto them, Moses because of the hardness of your hearts suffered you to put away your wives: BUT from the beginning it was not so. 9 And I SAY unto you, Whosoever shall put away his wife, except it be for fornication, and shall marry another, committeth adultery: and whoso marrieth her which is put away doth commit adultery.*

Notice first of all that Jesus used both the words fornication and adultery in His response. If fornication in this context were meant to be used in the general term of immorality, there would be no need for Him to use the word adultery again.

Jesus knew exactly what He wanted to communicate when He made a distinction between the word fornication and adultery in His answer. As the God man, He did not need anyone to instruct Him on how to use words in their context. He is the living Word.

The term fornication used here is referring to the first part of the Jewish marriage which is the engagement period. This was considered to be stage one of a two part marriage process. That period is usually between six months to a year. This was brought out in *Luke 2:4-5 – 4 Joseph also went up from Galilee, out of the city of Nazareth, into Judaea, unto the city of David, which is called Bethlehem; (because he was of the house and lineage of David:) 5 To be taxed* **with Mary his espoused {engaged} WIFE**, *being great with child.*

Wikipedia Encyclopedia: Technically, the Jewish wedding process has two distinct stages. [1] The first, kiddushin (Hebrew for "betrothal"; sanctification or dedication, also called erusin) and nissuin (marriage), is when the couple start their life together. It is at the first stage (kiddushin) that the woman becomes prohibited to all other men, requiring a (religious divorce) to dissolve it, while the second stage permits the couple to 'intercourse with' each other. The ceremony that accomplishes nissuin is also known as chuppah.[2].

Holman Illustrated Bible Dictionary: …The biblical terms, betrothal and espousal, are almost synonymous with marriage and as binding. Betrothal and marriage comprised a moral and spiritual principle for the home and society. The penalty under the law of Moses for disrupting this principle by adultery, rape, fornication, or incest was death by stoning.

The old testament reference for this practice is *Deuteronomy 22:23-27 23. If a damsel that is a virgin be betrothed unto an husband, and a man find her in the city, and lie with her; 24. ye shall bring them both out unto the gate of that city, and ye shall stone them with stones that they die; the damsel, because she cried not, being in the city; and the man, because he hath humbled his neighbour's wife: so thou shalt put away evil from among you. 25. But if a man find a betrothed damsel in the field, and the man force her, and lie with her: then the man only that lay with her shall die: 26. But unto the damsel thou shalt do* *nothing; there is in the damsel no sin worthy of death: for as when a man riseth against his neighbour, and slayeth him, even so is this matter: 27. For he found her in the field, and **the betrothed damsel cried**, and there was none to save her.*

To emphasize that Jesus had never deviated from the position of that which was from the beginning, let us examine the following: Jesus, without any provocation, brought up the issue on His own terms in *Luke 16:18. "Whosoever putteth away his wife, and marrieth another, committeth adultery: and whosoever marrieth her that is put away from her husband committeth adultery."*

Examine Jesus' own mandates to the apostle Paul even after His ascension. *1 Corinthians 7:10-11 10. And unto the married I command, **yet not I, but the Lord,** Let not the wife depart from her husband: 11. But and if she depart, let her remain unmarried, or be reconciled to her husband: and let not the husband put away (divorce) his wife.*

Do you know what God's position is on divorce? He HATES it. *[Malachi 2:16] For the LORD, the God of Israel, saith that he hateth putting away (divorce): for one covereth violence with his garment, saith the LORD of hosts: therefore take heed to your spirit, that ye deal not treacherously.*

Ideally, death is a biblical basis for being loosed from a spouse. Examine *1 Corinthians 7:39 "The wife is bound by the law as long as her husband liveth; but if her husband be dead, she is at liberty to be married to whom she will; only in the Lord."*

Abandonment by the *unsaved spouse* is a biblical basis for being loosed from a spouse. This standard is brought out in *1 Corinthians 7:12-15. 12. But to the rest speak I, not the Lord: If any brother hath a wife that believeth not, and she be pleased to dwell with him, let him not put her away. 13. And the woman which hath an husband that believeth not, and if he be pleased to dwell with her, let her not leave him. 14. For the unbelieving*

29

husband is sanctified by the wife, and the unbelieving wife is sanctified by the husband: else were your children unclean; but now are they holy. 15. But if the unbelieving depart, let him depart. A brother or a sister is not under bondage in such cases: but God hath called us to peace.

Question: What if the two got married and divorced prior to coming to know Christ as Savior? Are they biblically loosed from a spouse?

Answer: This would be like asking if the unbelieving couple got saved and become a member of the church, would they be considered a legitimate couple after becoming a Christian?

Answer: The context of this passage is specifically discussing the *saved spouse whose unbelieving spouse abandoned him/her* because of his/her decision for Christ. If the two of them got saved, that is a different story.

The question as to whether adultery is being committed by remarriage after a divorce is inevitable, based upon, if I may say, the perfect will of God or God's ideal for marriage. However, as to which party causes it is another sin. Jesus tells us in *Matthew 5:31-32 "31. It hath been said, Whosoever shall put away his wife, let him give her a writing of divorcement: 32. But I say unto you, That whosoever shall put away his wife, saving for the cause of fornication, CAUSETH HER TO COMMIT ADULTERY: and whosoever shall marry her that is divorced committeth adultery."*

As was brought out before, both the word fornication and adultery were used in this passage also, which rules out the general use of fornication to apply to general immorality. If the context were pointing to general immorality, there would be no need for the word adultery. Our Lord's use of fornication and adultery has different meaning in the context of this passage. The word fornication used here is referring to the engagement or betrothal period of the Jewish marriage practice.

Marriage is an earthly transaction and we will not be classified by our earthly marital status when we get to heaven. However, the sins committed against the marriage will be remanded to the violators. Examine Jesus' answer to this question in *Matthew 22:25-30.* – *"25 Now there were with us seven brethren: and the first, when he had married a wife, deceased, and, having no issue, left his wife unto his brother: 26 Likewise the second also, and the third, unto the seventh. 27 And last of all the woman died also. 28 Therefore in the resurrection whose wife shall she be of the seven? for they all had her. 29 Jesus answered and said unto them, Ye do err, not knowing the scriptures, nor the power of God. 30 For in the resurrection they neither marry, nor are given in marriage, but are as the angels of God in heaven.*

How should we behave in marriage regarding intimacy? Neither spouse should deprive the other of what is due them in marriage. The apostle Paul stipulated this standard in *1 Corinthians 7:3-4* – *"3 Let the husband render unto the wife due benevolence: and likewise also the wife unto the husband. 4 The wife hath not power of her own body, but the husband: and likewise also the husband hath not power of his own body, but the wife."*

This is calling for a mutual inter-resolve to please each other intimately. This mandate specifically leveled the playing field, whereas neither of the parties has superior powers in this matter. Both are to resolve to please each other.

The writer of the book of Hebrews reinforces this fact but from a more positive perspective in *Hebrews 13:4.* It says: *Marriage is honourable in all, and the bed undefiled: but whoremongers and adulterers God will judge.*

Yes, this is a license to be as creative as you would like or as you can but never abusive. I would even dare to say that it is recommended to be creative, as long as you both agree. I would even be obliged to say that variety in the planned diet of intimacy could be a great diet for the marriage union.

However, consent must be mutual and then the bed is undefiled. The only limit "with each other" is when it crosses the line of abuse. It crosses the line of abuse when there is not mutual consent and when it crosses into hurting each other or one party.

Neither spouse should depart from the other without consent. This mandate is stipulated in *1 Corinthians 7:5. "Defraud ye not one the other, except it be with consent for a time, that ye may give yourselves to fasting and prayer; and come together again, that Satan tempt you not for your incontinency (lack of self-restraint).*

Adam Clarke's Commentary: Defraud ye not one the other— What ye owe thus to each other never refuse paying, unless by mutual consent; and let that be only for a certain time, when prudence dictates the temporary separation, or when some extraordinary spiritual occasion may render it mutually agreeable, in order that ye may fast and pray, and derive the greatest possible benefit from these duties by being enabled to wait on the Lord without distraction.

Barnes' Notes on the New Testament: Defraud ye not - Of the right mentioned above, withdraw not from the society of each other except it be with consent. It must be with a mutual understanding that you may engage in the extraordinary duties of religion.

Tony Evans Bible Commentary: Husbands and wives are to protect one another from sin by not depriving one another. The only exception to regular sexual intimacy is when the couple agrees to a limited time period in which they devote themselves to prayer and fasting. We might refer to this as "sexual fasting." To fast is to temporarily give up satisfying a craving of the body in order to focus and give extra attention to a spiritual need. If a husband and wife need God to intervene in a situation, a sexual fast for the purpose of prayer is in order.

The word defraud used here is a legal or judiciary term used in criminal or civil proceedings which means to *deprive*, be destitute, kept back by fraud. To defraud or deprive is only allowed here by consent or there must be consensus. It is only allowed for spiritual devotion and commitment and it must be temporary. The delicate plumb-line for this caution is to circumvent incontinence (*lack of self-restraint*).

CHAPTER 3

Are You in Love With a Body or a Being?

Yes, what you see is not always what you get!
What you get is what you may not have seen.
The surface is just a cover. Dare to open the lid
and see inside.

The Beauty Within First Beauty

I'm truly in love with beauty
I've always searched for it
But then I met you Cutie
And was drawn beyond your fit

If I were to check first beauty
I'd give you triple-A plus
But I found in you a beauty
That goes far beyond your dust

There's a beauty within first beauty
For that, I've found in you
My love is for that beauty
And nothing else will do

To you I'll pay my duty
To you I'll humbly bow
With you I'll sign love treaty
With you I'll make my vow

Are you engaging in a relationship with a being or are you madly in love with a body to the extent that you totally ignore the being? What you see on the outside is just a shell that covers the real being of which, if you dare to venture to 'see,' is the real adventure that you will get, regardless of what you are seeing outwardly.

Be careful that you don't fall into the time bomb of falling in love with the the 'triple b' instead of the person? A careful examination of the so called love relationships today reveals that our culture is in love with the 'triple b' instead of the being or the person. *The* 'triple b' *are the body, beauty and bulge.*

How important are the 'triple b' to a lasting love relationship? Ok... I concede that there must be the "wow factor" or this baby cannot even pass through your entrance door. However, the real question is what happens after that person has passed through your entrance door and is now at least in your thoughts or more so, has found a way into your heart? This relentlessly intriguing venture is a ticking time bomb when the three b's are all that matter to you while there is a real being who is truly the person who occupies that shell.

People usually get their high on their prospects 'triple b' and refuse to come down until they are forced to do so by the realities of life or a rejection from the other party. It feels good, it seems good, it taste good and that appears to be all that usually matters in this honeymoon period.

Anyone who dares to interrupt this adrenaline flow is usually resisted and to a greater extent rejected at times, regardless of the position that they held in this person's life prior to this encounter. Family members are not excluded, regardless of whether they are immediate or distant.

An authority on family issues likened this high to a state of intoxication of the highest order. It consumes and holds one captivated for an undetermined period of time. If this is your take or price, it usually only takes one with a set of 'triple b' of a more captivating order or intruding consequences of a very stern order to break that cycle. In many instances, the only means of interrupting that high is a divine intervention.

The wow factor by itself usually is not a lasting element in a love relationship. If allowed to take its unhealthy course, it usually ends involuntarily by at least one of the parties. This usually happens after the honeymoon phase expires and the real person shows up.

After the "wow factor" fueled by the 'triple b', then what? After we are captivated by this person's 'triple b', we usually resort to one of the 'triple m' postures in our relationships.

We usually assume one of three postures towards all of the other qualities of that person, which are in actuality, the real qualities that will determine true lasting possibilities.

The first posture that we usually assume during the "wow factor" is the *minimization* posture. In this posture, whether the other qualities of this person are commendable or despicable, we minimize their importance and the importance of acknowledging that person for who they really are, and continue to maximize the importance of their 'triple b'. We major on the 'triple b' and minor on the other important and real qualities of that person.

A deeper dilemma to this illogical and most of all, spiritually deficient relationship is to not even acknowledge the need to become acquainted with these non-'triple b' qualities of that person. To the instigator and facilitator, they are not even necessary because he/she is now feeding off the "wow factor" namely, the other person's 'triple b'.

That's all that matters, that's all that will ever matter, they conclude. What about the other undiscovered qualities of that person (good or bad) that may pop up later and haunt this relationship or may be responsible for the promotion, perpetuation and preservation of this relationship? Aren't you the least bit concerned about the presence or absence of these qualities?

Do you really know that person in whole or do you just know, and only want to know their 'triple b'? At times, the party with the 'triple b' that is fueling the emotional high, cannot even be held fully responsible for the imminent deception of the facilitating party. Quite often, the facilitating party on their own has already coined an image that they want that person to be and has already convinced themselves that the fueling party is that image, without proper investigation or existing evidence.

If 'triple b' are your primary or sole criterion for getting involved in a committed relationship, you are engaged in a serious emotional enslavement or potential roller coaster, because the possibilities are endless in that arena. You will always find a 'seems better' or apparently more attractive prospect. With the current availability of beauty oriented enhancements and today's high level of fitness consciousness, you could virtually find your triple b', apparent ideal in just about every opposite sex that you meet.

News Flash: There is a whole new world of qualities that exist about that person which are probably more complex, more interesting and are of greater importance to a lasting relationship than their 'triple b'. Your boldness to go beyond the 'triple b' and explore that other world now could save you a world of surprises that are waiting in the balance there for your near or far tomorrow.

Believe it or not, you may like that other world more than you like the triple b'. And if you don't, so what, much credit to you now for facing reality. Believe it or not, this is a Ripley's… it would be far more difficult if you waited and figured that out in marriage.

The second posture that we usually assume during the "wow factor" is the *makeover* posture. Somehow we convinced ourselves that we can reverse seventeen, twenty, thirty years or more of being John Doe. The alarming factor is that we believe that we can accomplish this in the small compressed period of time that we want to cram all of our expectations in this fallible or fully developed person.

Instead of getting to know who that person really is, we resort to our intense campaign of demanding of that person what they must now become or else; against who they really are. Instead of giving that person the freedom to be who they really are and let them hang themselves or raise themselves to be our ideal, we interrupt the pure process of exposure, corrupt the evidence and run away with a dead case that is filled with contamination and will not stand up in the court of marriage.

People are very good actors, especially when they are benefiting from the situation. If you tell them or show them how you want them to operate to stay in this relationship, you would be surprise how long some people will play their roles just to maintain their benefits.

Women are very good at that, but more so the men. As a matter of fact, most men have made it their strategy to play the role, tell you what you want to hear, give you what you want to get etc, until that ultimate objective is achieved. Then you are now added to their list of trophy as they move on other prizes.

The makeover approach can lead to the instigator reading into the behavior of the other party what they have predetermined their ideals should be without any evidence that that is so. As such, they read in and without evidence, come to a premature conclusion of the intentions and outcomes of the other party's actions with what they have now fictionalized as facts. As a result, even though the signs of a despicable behavior were conspicuous, they were not able to effectively identify them or face up to those facts.

In the makeover approach, you want to be careful what you ask for or what you have now hired. Usually in the makeover approach, you are paying for this fictionalized behavior with something that is unhealthy to a lasting relationship because you have to continue to supply that pacifier to maintain that fantasy.

A makeover approach always shortchanges at least one, if not both parties in the relationship. When you as the makeover instigator project or accept a fictionalized image that you desire, in the other party, you actually are facilitating the suffocation of the real person under that false image.

Have you heard of the young man who reluctantly sat down after multiple stern warnings from his parents to sit down? His response was, "I am sitting down on the outside but I am standing up on the inside." A projected or accepted makeover behavior could create a monstrous partner like that young man.

Counterfeits cannot be counterfeits forever, only truth can operate in that light. By this, I am saying that the true person will come out at an interval. When that true behavior comes out, is it going to be a snake that you have been covering up under the grass or a sweet person that you have been suppressing by your projected or accepted demands for an image that does not really exist?

Instead of the makeover approach, an approach that gives the person the freedom to be their true self is the greater investment in a lasting relationship. An approach where both parties seek to find out what are the person's likes and dislikes; how the person operates under situations of having total control and situations of involuntary loss and pressure is highly revealing.

An approach where that person does not feel threatened or pressured into certain false expectations is highly fact finding. If you allow the person to be their true self where you can see how they would operate when they are on their guard and when they are off guard is also truly fact finding.

The third posture that we usually assume during the "wow factor" is the *measuring* posture. Believe it or not, this posture is the most sobering posture of the three. The courtship period is a period of investigation and affirmation. It is a time to investigate the qualities in the other person, whether they be good or bad and affirm that this person with these qualities did meet the standards that you have previously established for your mate.

Measuring your standards or perspectives on life with that person's and affirming that their standards and perspectives on life meet yours and yours meet theirs is what courtship is all about. The courtship period is classified as the *silent detective period*. Silent, in that you are not looking for reasons to accuse but to rule out or

40

rule in. Detective, in that it is a mission to find the real person. It is during the courtship period that you want the real person to stand up, not in the marital period.

Believe it or not, this is not a time to impress and put the best outside as it is a time of being yourself even the more. The other party should afford you the opportunity of seeing them as they really are and vice versa. If they don't voluntarily grant you that privilege, then you must be both patient and tactfully skillful enough to pull it out or wait the course until you receive reasonable assurance that your mission is accomplished.

Deliberate *measurement* should be made in relation to the compatibility factors of each other, the conducive nature of each others' dreams, goals or mission in life. At the top of this arena is ones spiritual or divine calling. Are their dreams, goals or mission in life going to conflict with or complement the calling of God on your life or in any way cast a shadow over it? Are they making demands of you that are stifling your primary mission in life or God's calling upon your life?

Are you both able to carry out each of your life's mission and still function in harmony? If the answer is no, there is a red flag waving, or at least an amber flag.

Measurement should be made in relation to the compatibility or conflicts of your values and standards as a person. This relates to your human values and standards as a person. Foremost among your primary concerns should be your spiritual values and standards as a Christian. Someone said that there are certain values and standards that are non-negotiable and your spiritual values and standards should be at the top of that list. Do you have any predetermined non-negotiables? You will achieve greater success if you have those non-negotiables as predetermined resolves rather than making them up as you go along.

In *measuring* the compatibility or conflict of yours or our prospect's spiritual values and standards, it is important that you observe their association: Their social hangouts or places and companies that they want to take you. It is important that you take note of their music and language to see if there exists a compatibility or a conflict in both of you being able to harmonize these values. If the answer is no, there exists a red flag or at least an amber flag.

CHAPTER 4

Do not Contaminate but Construct the Evidence

A case that's built on assumption rather than uncontaminated evidence will fail under the scrutiny of the courts (marriage). You cannot construct the evidence at the trial; it must be done pretrial.

Attention: Just because a person is available and you are available, does not necessarily mean that that person is for you or you for that person. The quest to an accurate or appropriate determination of the truth of this mystery goes far beyond the point of your first hello or the day that you first laid eyes on each other.

The answer to the question of "what is your partner's or prospect's relationship background and aptitude" is the puzzle that this discussion seeks to divulge. The quote that warns us to know our history or we are bound to repeat it is a profoundly true statement that is applicable to the ability, or lack thereof of your prospect effectively sustaining a lasting relationship with you. So, in your quest for the true identity of your partner or partner to be, you must endeavor to ascertain both your prospect and his/her parents' relationship background and its aptitude.

While you resolve to observe and record (retain) your prospect's background and relationship aptitude, this process must be comprised of some key entities.

First, you must seek to ascertain the level of your prospect's ability to release himself/herself and resources to you and others more than they are seeking to receive. Does he/she have the ability to take the camera off themselves and focus it on you as well as others and not feel robbed?

Furthermore, is that person able to snap your pictures and those of others, focus on them, highlight all of their qualities without worrying about himself/herself being left out? Is it all about him/her or is it about both of you? Furthermore, how much of his/her interaction with you is about or focused on you? Your findings in this quest could reveal whether you are about to be involved in a relationship that is "one way" bound or a relationship enriched with positive reciprocity.

Positive reciprocity is responding to a positive action with another positive action or rewarding kind actions with kind actions. It is also responding to a negative action with a positive one and thus not rewarding negative actions. You need to record how much of your acts of kindness is met with acts of kindness or a response with conscious means of consistent withdrawals from your personal bank. That is a revelation of what your journey with this person will be like. Is this person's method of accommodating a relationship one which builds you up or pulls you down? Can and does this person celebrate your achievements and successes or feels intimidated by them?

According to the older folks, it takes two hands to clap. The point of this proverb that is applicable to this discussion is that when one hand is raised to give a high five or to support one's efforts, there must be another hand that is raised to meet it or there will be no music, so to speak.

Secondly, the question of a self or others centered approach to relationships also extends into you ascertaining the level of your prospect's ability to appropriately accept self induced blame instead of ascribing it to both you and others. Does he/she always project that you or others fail when he/she fails; or does he/she accurately or appropriately deal with failure and take responsibility for same?

44

Dare to open the lid and see inside

Thirdly, you must seek to ascertain the level of your prospect's ability to handle conflicts. Do they seek to discuss or negotiate or do they seek to argue, attack and raise their voices for minor points of differences of opinion? Do they approach conflict strategically and are willing to seek adequate solutions, even if it involves outside help or help from another person, if necessary? Most of all, are they willing to seek and apply the Lord's take on the issue or situation?

Do they seek to maintain self sufficiency even to the death of the relationship? Do they push you to do the same so that 'their' ego can stand intact even when it is time to seek advice or seek help, especially God's? On the other hand do they crumble at the touch of a rumble? Are they able to recover from a setback in a reasonable or record time period or are they prone to stay, dwell on or wallow in defeat or blame?

Fourthly, you should seek to ascertain both your prospect's and their parents' relationship background or history. Like someone rightly said, if you want to see what your husband is going to be like, look at his father at that same interval and if you want to see what your wife is going to be like, look at her mother at the same interval also.

Though this is not always so, it is the author's position that it is the Norm; the alternative outcome is the exception. Your role is to take note of relationship killers that were present in the parents' relationship diary that potentially will show up in that person's relationship with you.

How long and well were his parents able to maintain their relationship that potentially will show up in the offspring with you? This includes how easily or vigorously were they able to give up on or fight for their relationship, which may show up in their relationship with you.

How eager are they or their parents to share with others? Are they or their parents able to evenly share the truth even at their own expense or the expense of their child? To what grandeur

45

are they and their parents' ambitions to foster theirs, their children's interests over others unjustifiably; and where on their ranking chain does yours or others' interest fit in?

Fifthly, When you examine the structure of their spiritual house, where has it been, where is it currently and where do the 'actions' and lifestyle show that it is heading? What one practices, that he will become, regardless of what he thinks he is or will be. Is the 'God idea' a dismal effort of stretch to fit into their lifestyle or is there a genuine embracing and convincing commitment to the God lifestyle? In a real sense, you can determine that by what they want to do, where they want to go... more so, where they end up going and what they end up doing, irrespective of what they say or are trying to portray.

Sixth, you must seek to ascertain whether your prospect is 'complementive' or destructive in his/her relationship strategy? Does he/she assume an overly critical posture in their relationship strategy? Jesus gave the best measuring rod in this matter. His discourse in *John 10:10 says "The thief cometh not, but for to steal, and to kill, and to destroy: I am come that they might have life, and that they might have it more abundantly."*

Has your prospect come into your life to take from you or to give (contribute) to you? Has he/she come into your life to destroy you or to protect and preserve you and your ambitions? Has he/she come into your life to build you up and complement you and your mission or has he/she come to be a liability, to bring you down and to destroy you and your potential? A relationship that is wrapped up in the mission and the spirit of Jesus Christ is one that reflects a spiritually abundant living and joy in each other's life.

Does your prospect have a questionable family background with a history of negative relationship aptitude? Does his/her current spiritual aptitude outweigh his questionable or negative relationship history? Does he/she have a consistent 'recordable' and 'sustained' positive spiritual aptitude that has become a lifestyle or a way of life for an extended period of time? That is indicative of a genuine spiritual change of heart and life?

46

Dare to open the lid and see inside

Has he/she shown 'sustained' signs of renouncing his/her questionable family background and negative relationship aptitude? Furthermore, do the signs show that he/she has been embracing the Word of God, the way of God and the will of God as a way of life or a lifestyle?

Is the magnitude of the evidence of spiritual change reflective of a person who will likely maintain a lasting relationship or otherwise? You must seek God's eyes and wisdom in your conclusion with this because your own wisdom cannot appropriately determine the right conclusion.

Regardless of how capable you may rate your wit in this matter, *Proverbs 3:5-6* must be invoked in your ultimate strategical endeavor to tie the bow on this gift. It implores us to *"5 Trust in the LORD with all thine heart; and lean not unto thine own understanding. 6 In all thy ways acknowledge him, and he shall direct thy paths."* Much pray and fasting are necessary to wrap up this bow.

Since we all have at least some form of a questionable and negative background, we must approach this venture with serious humility and unflinching embracing of the wisdom of God as we seek the will of God. We must also resolve within ourselves that since our level of spiritual aptitude is that which does not on our own, surpass all of our questionable and negative background, it is the full embracing of and commitment to a high level of spiritual aptitude that will achieve a lasting relationship for all of us.

Who will be so gifted, so qualified, so 'lucky' if you please, so able and most of all so blessed to be worthy of your love for the rest of your life?

CHAPTER 5

The Ideal Wife or Woman

The Proverbs 31 Woman - The virtuous woman -
A good wife or woman Proverbs 31:10-31

THE IDEAL WOMAN

She's a lady within a lady
She's a heart within a heart
She spreads out to give you shady
From within her inward part

She's a woman of tending caliber
She's a vision of sending ranks
And her love is like a river
That flows within her banks

It ascends to the high and mighty
It descends to the weak and low
In meekness it runs and cites thee
Like an arrow thumbed from her bow

May the good Lord bless and keep her
And supply her every need
May His loving wings spread over
And protect her cherry seed

Dedicated to Cynthia Scott, whose life has been a living Bible
and has reached out and helped countless numbers of needy folks

who have come her way, including me (Gilbert James)

As we examine this biblical template for the ideal wife or woman, there are a few preliminary factors that must be set down from the outset.

One: This image of a virtually perfect wife, as presented in this passage, was not born out of a wife or woman tooting her own horn but was originated from a potential mother-in-law counseling her son regarding what he should consider an ideal wife or woman. This truth is established in *Proverbs 31:1 The words of king Lemuel, the prophecy that his mother taught him.*

Two: Ladies, wives, if you want to have your mother-in-law going off the chain about you, then pay very close attention to the characteristics of this ideal wife that mamma expects for her boy. Look at how she see her baby boy: *Proverbs 31:2 What, my son? and what, the son of my womb? and what, the son of my vows?*

Three: Warning - A virtuous woman will most likely train her son whether directly or indirectly (out-rightly or by observation) to look for a virtuous woman. Here is what this potential mother-in-law tells her son: *Proverbs 31:3 Give not thy strength unto women, nor thy ways to that which destroyeth kings.*

By this she warns him: Do not ever relinquish your *dignity*, your *integrity*, your *honor*, your *manhood* to any woman. These, you must preserve not only at all times but at all cost.

If you are after your good man's *strength*, his *dignity*, his *integrity*, his *honor*, his *manhood*, says this potential mother-in-law; not only are you not a good woman for her son but you are not a good woman, period.

Four: Just in case, future daughters-in-law, you say that this is a phantom woman... she doesn't exist, Lumuel's mother represents at least one woman, because, for her to be training her son to look for this type of woman, she must, of necessity, have been one herself.

Dare to open the lid and see inside

If you want proof that this type of woman exists today, I can confirm that with at least one woman: my mother... she was one epitome of the characteristics of the virtuous woman outlined in proverbs 31.

Do you know of anyone in your life's experience who possesses the characteristics the virtuous woman described here? Ladies, can you accurately say that you are one of them?

As we examine this virtuous woman further, we will look at her self-worth. We will ascertain the answers to the following questions about her: Is a *"for sale"* sign written on her as we examine her lifestyle? How much does she cost or is she priceless? Is she the type that would settle for a lesser than what God wants for her or is she the type that shoots for the best of the best, spiritually?

In the first place, she is priceless: *Proverbs 31:10 Who can find a virtuous woman? for her price is far above rubies.*

This means that she is not for sale and she cannot be bought even with any sum of money or material goods that you may have or offer. She is not defined by a *hoochie mama* lifestyle or dressing profile, as if she is on the market and for sale at all times.

She is known for her intelligence, her wisdom, her smarts, her self worth, her ambition, her industriousness, her ability to edify and pour out herself into other people, including and especially her man and secondly her household.

She knows that she is well put together and beautiful in all her glory... as such. While maintaining and ever improving her outer beauty, she majors on promoting her inner beauty strengths above her outer. Her outer beauty and strengths are to her, the bonus while the inner are her true values. Look at what she imparted to her son to look for in his woman: *Prov. 31:30, Favour is deceitful, and beauty is vain: but a woman that feareth the LORD, she shall be praised.*

51

Her real value is incalculable. What makes this a bad situation for the male predator is that SHE KNOWS IT. *This truth is brought clearly in Proverbs 31:18 – She perceiveth that her merchandise is good.* This also includes her... Though this reflection is not explicit in the immediate context of the verse, it is supported by her overall demeanor.

She dresses for success. Proverbs 31:22 tells us the following: *She maketh herself coverings of tapestry; her clothing is silk and purple.*

Notice first of all that she is creative: she can make her own clothes. Notice secondly that she dresses with and in class. However, pay special attention to the fact that she does not pressure her husband to afford what neither he, nor the family can. What the family can't afford, she makes up for with her own industrial ambitious ventures. The lesson here is buy if you can, but get creative if you can't.

Tapestry is a form of textile art, traditionally woven by hand on a loom...Tapestry is weft-faced weaving, in which all the warp threads are hidden in the completed work, unlike most woven textiles, where both the warp and the weft threads may be visible. In tapestry weaving, weft yarns are typically discontinuous (unlike brocade); the artisan interlaces each coloured weft back and forth in its own small pattern area. It is a plain weft-faced weave having weft threads of different colours worked over portions of the warp to form the design. *—https:// en.wikipedia.org/wiki/Tapestry—*

Purple is the color of *royalty.* It is used in that form in *Judges 8:26 – And the weight of the golden earrings that he requested was a thousand and seven hundred shekels of gold; beside ornaments, and collars, and* **purple raiment that was on the kings of Midian,** *and beside the chains that were about their camels' necks.* This is also seen in *Mark 15:17 And* **they clothed him with purple, and platted a crown** *of thorns, and put it about his head,*

It is also a symbol of wealth and prosperity. This can be seen in *Luke 16:19 – "There was a certain rich man, which* **was clothed in purple** *and fine linen, and fared sumptuously every day:"*

She commands honor and respect in her demeanor and she builds a foundation for the future. She does not itch to, neither does she consume all of her resources in the here and now. This principle of the virtuous woman is supported by *Proverbs 31:25: Strength and honour are her clothing; and "she shall rejoice in time to come."*

Though you cannot put on strength or honor as a piece of clothing, the way that she carries herself sends that message loud and clear: *I am of great value... my value is incalculable!*

The contemporary term, "a strong woman" is indeed she, personified. What is meant by a strong woman here?

It doesn't mean that she sees herself independent of or superior to her husband. Verse eleven and twelve of proverbs 31 dispels that notion: *The heart of her husband doth safely trust in her, so that he shall have no need of spoil.* She *will do him good and not evil all the days of her life.*

"Strong woman" in the case of this virtuous woman does not mean that she sees herself aligning with any feminist clan which would negatively impact her husband or her household. *Prov. 31:15* and *21* confirm that. *15 She riseth also while it is yet night, and giveth meat* **to her household**, *and a portion to her maidens. 21 She is not afraid of the snow* **for her household**: *for* **all her household** *are clothed with scarlet.*

A strong woman for this virtuous woman doesn't mean that she sees herself independent of God, quite the opposite. Look at what the mother of king Lemuel (Solomon) trained him to look for in his woman's vertical barometer: *Prov. 31:30, Favour is deceitful, and beauty is vain: but a woman that feareth the LORD, she shall be praised.* It is fair to say that among the characteristics of a virtuous woman for Solomon's mother, the top priority would be that she fears the Lord. In order for them to have a horizontal relationship, the vertical must first be set in place in her life.

How does she classify favor (popularity or the approval of the human species) compared to a relationship with God? She placed that in the deceitful category. This means that to her, it is selfish, deceptive, relative and temporary. How does she classify beauty compared to a relationship with God? It is empty, pure shell, unsatisfying self serving when its glory is found in itself alone, instead of God..

Notice that she does not give herself time to be depressed, she picks herself up and goes. Examine what is said of her posture in *Proverbs 31:17 She girdeth her loins with strength, and strengtheneth her arms.* This woman's approach to potential or actual disappointments mirrors the heart of king David who "encouraged himself in the Lord his God *1 Samuel 30:6 And David was greatly distressed; for the people spake of stoning him, because the soul of all the people was grieved, every man for his sons and for his daughters: but **David encouraged himself in the LORD his God.***

Examine the virtuous woman's relationship with her husband. In the first place, she seeks to do him good instead of harm. *Proverbs. 31:12 She will do him good and not evil all the days of her life.* Notice the duration of her lifestyle of doing 'good' to her husband: all the days of her life. The banner that she carries for her husband is to do him good for as long as she lives.

Notice that this accolade was not coming from her. She does not have to toot her own horn, her works spoke volumes... they spoke for themselves. Her own husband affirmed that fact: **He calls her blessed** in *Proverbs 31:28 Her children arise up, and call her blessed; her husband also, and he praiseth her.* Notice also that to her husband, she was praiseworthy. Her lifestyle remanded that.

Secondly, she prepares adequate food for her husband: I can hear some of the men saying at least silently, AMEN! *Proverbs 31:15* tells us this for her: *She riseth also while it is yet night, and giveth meat to her household, and a portion to her maidens.* Notice that she cooks and serves adequate food to her maidens (maids) when it should be the other way around. It seems like this virtuous woman doesn't trust the consumables of her household to her maids. She handles that herself. You never know what might *accidentally* slip into those meals. *Lol*

In our present society, sometimes the wife is the one out all day depending on the situation at home. Should the husband wait for her to come home and still cook or should he do the honors if he can? Should the husband help out in the kitchen even when both of them are at home?

In the third place, this virtuous woman tends to her husband's clothes. She ensures that he goes out the door looking good. Look at what is said of her husband's appearance under her watch: *Proverbs. 31:23 – Her husband is known in the gates, when he sitteth among the elders of the land.* She made sure that when her husband goes out into the public, he dresses for success as she does.

In the fourth place, she, that is the virtuous woman is a symbol of security for her husband. He trusts her and he dwells in safety with her: *Proverbs 31:11 – The heart of her husband doth safely trust in her, so that he shall have no need of spoil.* He, that is her husband, comes home to safety instead of nagging. She provided no grounds for him to question her motives or ulterior objectives towards him, quite the opposite.

Let us also observe, especially us men, that her husband's treatment of her played a vital role in her success as well. The above passage tells us that he, that is her husband, *trusts* her.

This also means that he doesn't micro manage her in everything that she does. To the contrary, he gives her freedom to be creative and be all that she can be. This means that he allows her to be co-contributor to the decision makings and as such, co-owner of the outcomes. He also compliments or praises her in her endeavors according to *Proverbs 31:28 Her children arise up, and call her blessed;* **her husband also, and he praiseth her.**

This also shows that he sees no need to become suspicious of her in any way. I wonder if this is a credit to the virtuous woman who gave him no reason to suspect her? Is this also showing that her lifestyle was trustworthy?

The word "spoil" in *Proverbs 31:11* means "Prey." By this, we can gather that he does not see her as a predator, neither does he see her as a prey.

It means that he does not attack her person, he compliments her person in words and in action. Her husband is able to trust her because he knew that she was not for sale. Therefore, she first earned his trust by setting her price above money or materials according to *Proverbs 31:10 Who can find a virtuous woman? for her price is far above rubies.*

This virtuous woman's trustworthiness was not only seen through her husband's treatment of her, but first through her treatment of him. He knew that she does him good instead of harm: *Proverbs 31:12 She will do him good and not evil all the days of her life.*

He, that is her husband, sees her above every other woman and if I may say, *he only sees her w*hen it comes to his personal choice. It's as though if he had it to do all over again, he would choose the same woman. Listen to how he classified her in *Proverbs 31:29 Many daughters have done virtuously, but thou excellest them all.*

Her husband continuously builds her up with compliments and affirmation. Look at what *Proverbs 31:28* tells us that the husband does to her*: ...he praiseth her.* Husbands, compliments are always appropriate and usually appreciated. It is virtually never inappropriate to compliment. Men, *compliment!*

56

compliment! compliment! This is a sure way into her heart!

Her work habit can be summed up in one consistent theme: SHE WORKETH WILLINGLY WITH HER HANDS! She is not afraid to put her hand to the spindle. *Prov. 31:13, 19 13 She seeketh wool, and flax, and worketh willingly with her hands. 19 She layeth her hands to the spindle, and her hands hold the distaff.*

Her first place of work, her base, her heartbeat, her whys, is her household. She pours out everything from that perspective. She brings food from afar back to her base which is her household. We see this as a consistent lifestyle of the virtuous women in *Proverbs 31:14-15, 21, 27-28 14 She is like the merchants' ships; she bringeth her food from afar. 15 She riseth also while it is yet night, and giveth meat to **her household**, and a portion to her maidens. 21 is not afraid of the snow for **her household:** for all **her household** are clothed with scarlet. 27 She looketh well to the ways of **her household**, and eateth not the bread of idleness. 28 Her children arise up, and call her blessed; her husband also, and he praiseth*

Secondly, from the above passage, she is not timid about navigating her way around the savviest merchants of her day. In other words, she was running a successful business quite possibly from her home. However, it isn't far fetched to conclude from the passage that she had a business that was based outside of her house. She at least, likely, was an avid business traveler.

She sought materials to clothe her family and it was also clear that she also did such to turnover and make a profit with them. *Proverbs 31:13 She seeketh wool, and flax, and worketh willingly with her hands.*

She was very shrewd, or if one should say, gifted at examining well the profitability of a field or an investment, before she invests in it. This is seen in *Proverbs 31:16 She considereth a field, and buyeth it: with the fruit of her hands she planteth a vineyard.*

She was very innovative. Examine what is said about her creatiity in *Proverbs 31:24 She maketh fine linen, and selleth it; and delivereth girdles unto the merchant.*

She was extremely talented and gifted. Her products spoke for themselves in the public arena. Examine *Proverbs 31:31 -- Give her of the fruit of her hands; and let her own works praise her in the gates.* The gates here refers to the public arena or the place of commerce.

She had a portion of her harvest and her profit set aside for the needy. We see this truth in *Proverbs 31:20 She stretcheth out her hand to the poor; yea, she reacheth forth her hands to the needy.* Take note that this wasn't a plan-less frivolous distributor of her and her husband's hard earnings. To the contrary, she setup a budget for charity as well. This also is evidence that she likely had the other categories of their budgeting in tact.

In all of this, she was a tower of wisdom, approachable, and gave wise counsel. Look at what *Proverbs 31:26 says about her: She openeth her mouth with wisdom; and in her tongue is the law of kindness.*

"Men" Intimacy For The Woman Is In The Mind

Intimacy for the woman starts in the mind, not in the bedroom. As a matter of fact, intimacy for the woman starts and ends in the mind.

Treat the woman's mind and you will have her emotions and her body following. If you did not treat her mind, then you did not have her in the bedroom; **you simply took her**.

There are three basic roads to a woman's mind and they are found in this simple acronym: *W.T.T.*

☙

WORDS: Words are golden to a woman, more than we men

58

realize. If we do, it can have us well on our way to finding out the true secret of a woman. Effective word use for the woman comes in C.A.P.

COMPLIMENTS OR PRAISE is not only a stabilizer to a woman but it is her assurance or compass. It lets her know that what she is doing or has done is appreciated and she should continue doing same. A woman's antenna is always up yearning or searching for a signal from her man as to how she is doing. compliments or praise lets her know that she is doing well and propels her to keep it up. When you as her man take the initiative to compliment or praise her, you can take the credit for assuring and propelling her into the right direction. If you do not take that initiative, another man may, and earn the credit which should have been yours. Too many outside compliments or praise from another man, with the absence of yours, could spell disaster.

The husband of the *proverbs 31* woman found that out quite well. Look at how he treats his wife in *Proverbs 31:28 Her children arise up, and call her blessed; her husband also, and he PRAISETH HER. THAT IS COMPLIMENTING HER.* It is almost always appropriate to compliment, which is to say that it is almost never inappropriate to compliment. compliments are like pouring water on fire.They are also like pouring water or fertilizer on the root of the plant.

AFFIRM, which for a woman is like fuel added to the fuel tank of a vehicle. The woman needs affirmation to keep going, like a vehicle needs fuel to keep operating. Consider all the other extremely expensive and extremely valuable parts of a vehicle, which could be perfectly in tact while it shuts down on you in the middle of the road, simply because it ran out of gas or fuel. Look at how her husband affirms her in Proverbs 31:28: *Her children arise up, and CALL HER BLESSED; HER HUSBAND ALSO, and he praiseth her.* Can you imagine how many ways he used the word blessed to his wife? You are a *blessed* woman! God *bless* you! You are ever a *blessing* to me! You are a blessing to our family! The list is endless!

He was a source of *POSITIVE MIRROR/REFLECTION* to her. Look at how he assures her in *Proverbs 31:29 Many daughters have done virtuously, but 'THOU EXCELLEST THEM ALL.'* This is how I see you and there is none that can match you to me. As I look at you, this is what I am seeing standing out or outstanding about you, and that's everything about you. *Attention Men:* This does not mean that you wouldn't gain big points if you pick specific areas or anatomy of her to compliment. Lol

A woman has a few mirrors or reflections of herself that matter in her life which are (1) the mirror on the wall (2) the public (3) family and friends (4) you as her man who is in her inner circle (5) for the believers, the Word of God.

To determine what rank her man has among these five mirrors, I'll ask you this question: Why do you believe a woman will blatantly go against her parents mirror of her, her friends mirror of her, the mirror on the wall, or even the mirror of God's Word, at times and marry you? For the woman, the right man in her life, second to God, is the closest to her heart. At times, she even places him closer than God which should not be.

☙

TREATMENT: (1) Generosity (2) Care (3) Romance... this includes flowers, (4) Gentleness with her or being sensitive to her needs, these speak volume for the woman's well-being. I don't know why but from my experience, giving a woman flowers yield a whole lot of unexplained wonders in the man's corner.

The way that you treat her throughout the day pays big dividends in the bedroom. Did you talk to her nicely and address her with sweet, endearing or elevating terms throughout the day? Did you open the door for her? Did you help her in the kitchen or housework? Did you build her up with your words or did you tear her down or demean her?

Dare to open the lid and see inside

A very wise pastor told me that you start preparing her during the day or even days ahead for a wonderful experience in the bedroom. She will repay you back double times over in the bedroom.

My expansion on that is if you start preparing her throughout the day and she will repay you double times over in the bedroom, why not treat her that way ever or every day, and see if she likely will pay you back ever or every night in the bedroom?

℞

TOUCH: For the married man, there is no place that is off limits but that's a privilege that is only available to the married person. Men, (1) Embrace (2) Hugs (3) Holding hands (4) Kisses (5) Deliberate bounces in passing are like protein to the muscles of your relationship with your woman.

It isn't inappropriate to be deliberate about body connections or contacts with your woman. She will love and idolize you or that. This very much includes kissing. Sometimes just a body connection or contact, even though it may appear minimal to the physical eyes; speaks volumes in the economy of intimacy.

INDEX

65

M

N

worth 51

Y

you choose 15

your partner 14

Made in the USA
Columbia, SC
12 November 2024

45968415R00045